Frittata

Cook time: 30 minutes
Servings: 4
Cost per serving: $1.47

8 eggs
1/2 cup milk
1/2 cup diced onions
3 tablespoons olive oil
1 cup halved cherry tomatoes
1/4 cup parmesan
1 cup cooked chicken
Salt and pepper to taste

- Preheat oven to 350°F
- In a bowl, whisk eggs, milk, and seasoning
- Once combined, add cherry tomatoes, parmesan, and cooked chicken
- In a 10 inch cast iron skillet, heat oil and add onions, then cook for around 5 minutes
- Add egg mixture to skillet, and cook for 5-7 minutes
- Once edges start to pull away from the pan, put the skillet in the preheated oven and bake for 16-18 minutes

Breakfast Quesadillas

Cook time: 30 minutes

Servings: 1
Cost per serving: $1.19

2 eggs
Hot sauce to taste
Pinch of salt
⅓ cup cooked pinto beans or black beans, rinsed and drained
2 teaspoons butter or extra-virgin olive oil
1 tablespoon chopped onion
1 8 inch whole-grain tortilla
½ cup (packed) grated sharp cheddar cheese
Salsa (optional)

In a bowl, whisk the eggs with the hot sauce and salt until they are well blended. Add the beans and set aside.

Melt the butter in a medium-sized skillet over medium heat until it's bubbling. Pour in the egg mixture and cook, stirring often, until the eggs are just set, about 1 to 3 minutes. Transfer the mixture to a bowl to pause the cooking process (the eggs will finish cooking in the quesadilla). Stir in the onion.

In a separate, large skillet, warm the tortilla over medium heat, flipping occasionally. Once the pan and tortilla are warm, sprinkle one-half of the cheese over one-half of the tortilla. Top the cheese with scrambled eggs, then top the scrambled eggs with the remaining cheese. Press the empty tortilla half over the toppings.

Let the quesadilla cook until golden and crispy on the bottom, about 1 to 2 minutes, reducing the heat if necessary to prevent burning the tortilla. Flip it and cook until the second side is golden and crispy. Immediately remove the skillet from the heat and transfer the quesadilla to a cutting board. Let it cool for a few minutes to give it time to set, then serve immediately.

Three-Ingredient Pancakes

Cook time: 20 minutes
Servings: 2
Cost per serving: $0.45

1 large ripe banana
2 eggs
1/8 teaspoon baking powder
1 pinch ground cinnamon (optional)

    Mash banana in a bowl using a fork

    Add eggs, baking powder, and cinnamon and mix batter well

    In a greased skillet on medium heat, spoon batter into into heated pan and cook until bubbles form and the edges are dry, 2 to 3 minutes. Flip and cook until browned on the other side, 2 to 3 minutes.

    Repeat with remaining batter.

Overnight Oats

Cook time: 10 minutes
Servings: 1
Cost per serving: $1.72

- 1/2 cup oats
- 1/2 cup milk
- 1/2 cup yogurt
- 1 tablespoon honey (optional)
- 1 tablespoon chia seeds (optional)
- 1/2 cup frozen fruit of choice

> Put all of the ingredients in a sealable container
> Shake well to combine
> Let sit in the fridge overnight, 8 hours-3 days

Veggie Tater Tot Breakfast Bake

Cook time: 45 minutes
Servings: 8
Cost per serving: $1.03

- 1 pound frozen broccoli florets
- 1 medium diced red bell pepper
- 1/3 cup thinly sliced scallions
- 2 cups shredded sharp cheddar cheese

10 large eggs
1 cup milk
Salt and pepper to taste
1 (32-ounce) bag frozen tater tots

Arrange a rack in the middle of the oven and heat to 375°F. Coat a 9x13-inch baking dish with cooking spray; set aside.

Place the broccoli in a large microwave-safe bowl and microwave according to package directions until crisp-tender. (Alternatively, bring a large saucepan of water to a boil, add the broccoli, and cook until crisp-tender, about 3 minutes.) Drain well.

Transfer the broccoli to the baking dish in an even layer. Evenly sprinkle the red bell pepper, scallions, and 1 cup of the cheese over the broccoli. Place the eggs, half-and-half, and salt in a large bowl, season with pepper, and whisk until evenly combined. Pour over the broccoli mixture.

Arrange the tater tots in the baking dish side by side in a tight, single layer (you may have a few tater tots left over). Lightly coat the tater tots with cooking spray.

Bake 30 minutes. Sprinkle with the remaining 1 cup cheese. Bake until the eggs are set and the tater tots are crisp and golden-brown, 30 to 40 minutes more (metal pans will bake faster; check on the bake a few minutes early if using).

Let sit on a wire rack 10 minutes before serving.

Freezer-Friendly Breakfast Burritos

Cook time: 60 minutes

Servings: 12

Cost per serving: $0.81

2 medium Yukon gold potatoes, peeled and diced small

1 large red bell pepper, seeded and diced

1 small red onion, diced

1 tablespoon vegetable oil

Salt to taste

12 large eggs

1/4 cup milk (0.04)

2 tablespoons unsalted butter (0.19)

1 1/2 cups shredded Monterey Jack cheese (2.98)

12 (10- to 12-inch) flour tortillas (2.30)

> Heat the oven: Arrange a rack in the middle of the oven and heat to 400°F. Prepare space in the freezer for a baking sheet.
>
> Combine the potatoes, peppers, and onions together in a medium bowl. Drizzle with the oil and 1/2 teaspoon of the salt, and toss to coat. Transfer to an even layer on a baking sheet and roast until the potatoes are tender, about 20 minutes.

While the veggies roast, whisk together the eggs, milk, and remaining 1/2 teaspoon salt until combined. Melt the butter in a 10-inch skillet (cast iron or nonstick would be ideal) over medium heat. Add the eggs and cook, stirring occasionally, until mostly set but still moist, 4 to 5 minutes. Remove from the heat. Let the eggs and roasted vegetables cool while you set up an assembly station — the eggs and vegetables should be room temperature for best assembly. Tear off 12 squares of aluminum foil. Have your cheese and tortillas standing by. Place a tortilla on top of a piece of foil. Sprinkle 2 tablespoons of cheese onto the tortilla. Top the cheese with 1/4 cup roasted vegetables, followed by 2 heaping tablespoons of the scrambled eggs, and any extra toppings. Roll the burrito tightly by folding the sides over the filling, then rolling from the bottom up.

Wrap the burrito tightly in aluminum foil and repeat with filling and folding the remaining burritos. Freeze the burritos in a single layer on a baking sheet — they'll freeze faster and more uniformly this way. Store frozen burritos in a gallon-sized zip-top freezer bag for longer-term freezing.

Unwrap and microwave on high for 1 to 2 minutes, until warmed through, or heat in a regular or toaster oven at 350°F for 12 to 15 minutes.

Banana Flax Muffins

Cook time: 35 minutes
Servings: 6
Cost per serving: $0.33

- 3/4 cup mashed ripe bananas
- 1 large egg
- 2 tablespoon brown sugar
- 1/2 teaspoon vanilla
- 2 tablespoon olive oil
- 1 cup all-purpose flour
- 1 teaspoon baking powder
- 1/4 teaspoon salt
- 1/4 cup ground flaxseed
- 1/4 cup chopped walnuts (optional)

Preheat the oven to 425°F. In a medium bowl whisk together the mashed banana, egg, brown sugar, vanilla, and olive oil.

In a separate medium bowl, stir together the flour, baking powder, salt, flaxseed, and walnuts.

Pour the wet ingredients into the bowl of dry ingredients and stir them together just until no dry flour remains on the bottom of the bowl. Avoid over stirring the batter.

Line six wells of a muffin tin with paper liners, then divide the batter evenly between the six wells. It should fill the wells almost to the top. Transfer the muffins to the oven and bake at 425°F for five minutes, then reduce the heat setting to 350°F without opening the oven door, and bake for an additional 20 minutes. After baking, remove the muffins from the tin to allow them to cool. Enjoy the muffins immediately, or allow them to cool completely and then store in an air-tight container in the refrigerator.

Green Chile Migas

Cook time: 35 minutes
Servings: 4
Cost per serving: $1.18

6 corn tortillas
1/2 tablespoon cooking oil
2 tablespoon butter
8 large eggs
4 oz can diced green chiles
1/4 cup sour cream
2 ounces queso fresco or Monterey jack
2 green onions
Salt and pepper to taste

Preheat the oven to 400°F. Stack the tortillas and then cut them into six equal sized wedges. Place the tortilla wedges in a bowl and drizzle the cooking oil over top. Gently toss the tortillas until they are well coated in oil. Spread the oil coated tortilla triangles out over a baking sheet in a single layer. Bake the tortillas for 8-10 minutes, stirring once half way through, or until they are golden brown and crispy. Leave the oven turned on.

While the tortillas are baking, prepare the other ingredients. Lightly whisk the eggs, drain the can of green chiles, measure the sour cream, and slice the green onions. Also gather 2 Tbsp butter and 2 oz. queso fresco or shredded Monterey jack cheese.

Add the butter to a large skillet and heat over medium, or just below medium. Allow the butter to melt, then swirl the skillet to coat the bottom and around the edges. Pour the eggs into the hot skillet and gently scramble the eggs until they are about 60% solid (if you want to skip the oven and cook it all on the stove top, cook the eggs until they are about 85-90% solid). Season the eggs with a pinch of salt and pepper.

Take the eggs off the heat and spoon the green chiles over the surface. Add the sour cream in dollops all over the eggs. Add the baked tortilla chips and then gently fold them into the eggs so they are half covered beneath the eggs. Finally, crumble the queso fresco or sprinkle shredded Monterey jack over top.

Transfer the skillet to the oven (still set to 400°F) and bake for 5-8 minutes, or until the eggs are set and the cheese is melted. If cooking entirely on the stove top, place a lid on the skillet and place it over medium heat until the egg are fully set and the cheese is melted. Sprinkle sliced green onions over top just before serving

Ham and Cheese Biscuits

Cook time: 40 minutes
Servings: 6
Cost per serving: $0.80

2.5 cups all-purpose flour (plus a little for dusting)
Salt to taste
1/2 tablespoon sugar
4 teaspoon baking powder
1 pint heavy cream
6 slices cheese
12 slices deli ham

Preheat the oven to 400°F. In a large bowl combine the flour, salt, sugar, and baking powder. Stir until they are very well combined. Pour the heavy cream into the bowl and stir until all of the flour is moistened and a thick ball of dough forms.

Scrape the biscuit dough out of the bowl onto a well floured surface and press it down into a rough rectangle. Use a rolling pin to roll the dough out into a rectangle about 8x11 inches and about 1/2-inch thick. Cut the rectangle into 12 pieces.

Stack one slice of cheese and two slices of ham onto 6 of the biscuit squares, then top with the remaining 6 biscuit squares. Place the Ham and Cheese Biscuits onto a baking sheet covered in parchment paper and transfer to the preheated oven.

Bake the Ham and Cheese Biscuits for about 25 minutes, or until the biscuits are golden brown on top. Serve hot.

Southwest Scrambled Eggs

Cook time: 25 minutes
Servings: 4
Cost per serving: $1.53

- 8 large eggs
- 1/4 cup milk
- Salt and pepper to taste
- 1 tablespoon butter
- 15 ounces canned black beans
- 4 ounces diced green chiles
- 1/4 cup taco sauce
- 4 ounces pepper jack, shredded
- 2 green onions
- 1 small tomato

Rinse the can of beans in a colander and let drain as you prepare the eggs.

In a large bowl, combine the eggs, milk, a pinch of salt, and pepper. Whisk until fairly smooth. Heat a large skillet over medium-low heat. Once hot, add the butter and let it melt. Spread the butter over the surface of the skillet with a spatula. Pour the whisked eggs into the skillet and gently fold them with the spatula as they begin to set. Avoid over stirring the eggs. When the eggs are about 75% set (still soft, moist, and fluid around the edges), add the drained beans and chopped green chiles (no need to drain the chiles). Gently fold the beans and chiles into the scrambled eggs. Drizzle taco sauce over the eggs, then top with pepper jack. Place a lid on the skillet and let it warm for about 5 more minutes, or until the eggs are fully set and the cheese on top is melted.

While the eggs are warming through, slice the green onions and dice the tomato. Top the eggs with the fresh tomato and green onion just before serving.

Lindsay's Broccoli Cheddar

Cook time: 60 minutes
Servings: 4
Cost per serving: $1.95
1 tablespoon and 4 tablespoons unsalted butter, divided
1 sweet yellow onion, diced small
1 clove garlic, peeled and minced finely
1/4 cup all-purpose flour
2 cups low-sodium vegetable stock
2 cups milk
2 to 3 cups broccoli florets, diced into bite-size pieces
2 large carrots, trimmed, peeled, and sliced into very thin rounds
Salt and pepper to taste

> In a small saucepan, add 1 tablespoon butter, diced onion, and sauté over medium heat until the onion is translucent and barely browned, about 4 minutes.

Add garlic and cook for about 30 seconds, stirring constantly so it doesn't burn. Remove from heat and set pan aside.

In a large heavy-bottom pot add 4 tablespoons butter, flour, and cook over medium heat for about 3 to 5 minutes, whisking constantly, until flour is thickened.

Slowly add the vegetable stock, whisking constantly.

Slowly add the milk, whisking constantly. Allow mixture to simmer over low heat for about 15 to 20 minutes, or until it has reduced and thickened.

While mixture is simmering, chop broccoli and carrots. After simmering 15 to 20 minutes, add the broccoli and carrots.

Add the salt and pepper. Allow soup to simmer over low heat for about 20 to 25 minutes, or until it has reduced and thickened.

After simmering for about 20 to 25 minutes, add most of the cheese, reserving a small amount for garnishing bowls. Stir in cheese until melted and incorporated fully.

Transfer the soup to bowls, garnish with reserved cheese, and serve immediately.

Hot and Sour

Cook time: 35 minutes

Servings: 4

Cost per serving: $2.38

2 tablespoons vegetable oil, divided

1 tablespoon freshly grated ginger 4-5 garlic cloves, minced

8 cups vegetable broth

4 ounces shiitake mushrooms, stemmed and sliced

1 14 ounce block of firm tofu, drained, pressed, and cut into 1/2 inch cubes

1 medium bunch bok choy, sliced into strips

2 tablespoons white vinegar

Hot sauce to taste

1 tablespoons soy sauce

1 tablespoons granulated sugar

6 scallions, sliced

1/4 cup fresh cilantro, finely chopped

> Heat 1 tablespoon of oil in large saucepan over medium heat. Add ginger and garlic and sauté for about one minute, being careful to avoid burning.
>
> Add broth, raise heat, and bring to boil. Lower heat and add mushrooms, simmer for about ten minutes.
>
> While your broth simmers away, heat the remaining tablespoon of oil in large skillet over medium heat. Add tofu and cook on each side

until it begins to brown. Remove it from the pan and transfer to a plate.

Once the broth has simmered for ten minutes, stir in bok choy, vinegar, hot sauce, soy sauce and sugar. Simmer an additional ten minutes. Taste test the broth and adjust seasonings to your liking.

Add tofu into the broth, stir well, and remove from heat.

Stir in scallions and cilantro, setting just a bit of each aside.

Ladle the soup into bowls and top with remaining scallions and cilantro

Butternut Squash and Chicken

Cook time: 25 minutes

Servings: 2

Cost per serving: $1.85

1/2 diced yellow onion (0.39)

3 cloves minced garlic (0.13)

3 cups chicken broth (0.91)

1 pound pulled cooked chicken (1.00)

1 cup cooked rice (0.31)

1 cup butternut squash (0.48)

1 lemon (0.48)

Salt and pepper to taste

Brown onion and garlic in a pot, then add chicken broth. Bring to a simmer.
Dice 1 cup peeled butternut squash and add to the pot, let it cook for 10 minutes
Add chicken to the soup and once incorporated, add cooked rice
Add juice of 1 lemon and salt and pepper
Ladle the soup into bowls and, if desired, top with lemon slices

Red Lentil and Carrot

Cook time: 25 minutes

Servings: 2

Cost per serving: $0.75

1 white onion , finely sliced

2 teaspoons olive oil

3 garlic cloves, sliced

2 carrots , scrubbed and diced

85g red lentils

1 vegetable stock cube, crumbled

2 tablespoons chopped parsley

Put the kettle on to boil while you finely slice the onion. Heat the oil in a medium pan, add the onion and fry for 2 mins while you slice the garlic and dice the carrots. Add them to the pan, and cook briefly over the heat.
Pour in 1 liter of the boiling water from the kettle, stir in the lentils and stock cube, then cover the pan and cook over a medium heat for

15 mins until the lentils are tender. Take off the heat and stir in the parsley. Ladle into bowls, and scatter with extra parsley leaves, if desired

Chunky Vegetable and Brown Rice

Cook time: 60 minutes
Servings: 4
Cost per serving: $0.82

- 2 tablespoon olive oil
- 1 medium onion , halved and sliced
- 2 garlic cloves, finely sliced
- 2 celery sticks, trimmed and thinly sliced
- 2 medium carrots , cut into chunks
- 2 medium parsnips , cut into chunks
- 1 tbsp finely chopped thyme leaves
- 100g wholegrain rice
- 2 medium leeks , sliced
- Parsley to taste

Heat the oil in a large non-stick pan and add the onion, garlic, celery, carrots, parsnips and thyme. Cover with a lid and cook gently for 15 mins, stirring occasionally, until the onions are softened and beginning to colour. Add the rice and pour in 5 cups of cold water. Bring to the boil, then reduce the heat to a simmer and cook, uncovered, for 15 mins, stirring occasionally

Season the soup with plenty of ground black pepper and salt to taste, then stir in the leeks. Return to a gentle simmer and cook for a further 5 mins or until the leeks have softened. Adjust the seasoning to taste and blitz half the soup with a stick blender, leaving the other half chunky, if desired. Ladle into bowls, and top with parsley leaves, if desired

Sweet Potato and Lentil

Cook time: 35 minutes
Servings: 6
Cost per serving: $1.12

2 tsp medium curry powder
3 tbsp olive oil
2 onions, grated
1 apple, peeled, cored and grated
3 garlic cloves, crushed
1 ounce coriander seeds
Thumb-size piece fresh root ginger, grated
4 cups cooked sweet potatoes
5 cups low-sodium vegetable stock
1/2 cup red lentils
1 cup milk
Juice of 1 lime

Put the curry powder into a large saucepan, then toast over a medium heat for 2 mins. Add the olive oil, stirring as the spice sizzles in the pan. Add in the onions, apple, garlic, coriander and ginger, season, then gently cook for 5 mins, stirring every so often.

Meanwhile, peel, then grate the sweet potatoes. Add into the pan with the stock, lentils, milk and seasoning, then simmer, covered, for 20 mins. Blend until smooth using a stick blender. Stir in the lime juice, check the seasoning and serve, topped with roughly-chopped coriander leaves.

Carrot, Tarragon, and White Bean

Cook time: 30 minutes
Servings: 4
Cost per serving: $1.24
1 tbsp olive oil 2 large leeks , well washed, halved lengthways and finely sliced
5 1/2 cup carrots , chopped
6 cups vegetable stock
4 garlic cloves, finely grated
2 14 ounce cans cannellini beans in water
2/3 small pack tarragon , leaves roughly chopped

Heat the oil over a medium heat in a large pan and fry the leeks and carrots for 5 mins to soften

Pour over the stock, stir in the garlic, beans with their liquid, and three-quarters of the tarragon, then cover and simmer for 15 mins. Stir in the remaining tarragon before serving.

Classic Tomato

Cook time: 30 minutes
Servings: 4
Cost per serving: $0.76

2 tbsp olive oil 1 onion, chopped
1 garlic clove, finely chopped
1 tbsp tomato purée
14 ounce can chopped tomato
Dried basil to taste
Pinch of baking soda
2 1/2 cup milk

Heat the olive oil in a large pan, then add in the onion and garlic. Cook over medium heat until the onion has softened, about 5 mins. Stir in the tomato purée, then pour in the chopped tomatoes and basil leaves, and bring to a boil. Turn the heat down and leave to simmer for about 15 mins until thick

To finish the soup, tip the tomato mixture into a pan. Spoon the baking soda into a small bowl and pour over 1 tbsp or so of the milk. Mix together until there are no lumps, then add into the tomato mix and pour over the milk. Bring to a boil. Gently simmer for about 5 mins until ready to serve.

Chorizo and Chickpea

Cook time: 15 minutes
Servings: 2
Cost per serving: $1.25

- **14 ounce can chopped tomato**
- **1/2 cup chorizo sausage (unsliced)**
- **1/2 cup cabbage**
- **14 ounce can chickpeas, drained and rinsed**
- **1 chicken or vegetable stock cube**

Put a medium pan on the heat and tip in the tomatoes, followed by a can of water. While the tomatoes are heating, quickly chop the chorizo into chunky pieces (removing any skin) and shred the cabbage.

Add the chorizo and cabbage into the pan with the chilli flakes and chickpeas, then crumble in the stock cube. Stir well, cover and leave to bubble over high heat for 6 mins or until the cabbage is just tender. Ladle into bowls and eat with crusty or garlic bread if desired.

Minestrone

Cook time: 10 minutes
Servings: 4
Cost per serving: $0.69

4 cups hot vegetable stock
14 ounce canned chopped tomato
1/2 cup thin spaghetti, broken into short lengths
12 ounces frozen mixed vegetables
4 tbsp pesto
Drizzle of olive oil
Grated parmesan cheese to taste

> Bring the stock to a boil with the tomatoes, then add the spaghetti and cook for 6 mins or until done. A few minutes before the pasta is ready, add the vegetables and bring back to the boil. Simmer for 2 mins until everything is cooked
>
> Serve in bowls drizzled with pesto and oil, sprinkled with parmesan

Ramen Coleslaw

Cook time: 15 minutes
Servings: 5
Cost per serving: $0.98

- 16 ounce bag coleslaw mix
- 1 cup sunflower seeds
- 1 cup sliced almonds
- 2 3 ounce instant ramen packages, any flavor
- 5 green onions, sliced
- 3/4 cup vegetable oil
- 1/3 cup white vinegar
- 1/2 cup sugar

In a large bowl, place coleslaw mix, sunflower seeds, sliced almonds, crushed ramen, and scallions

In a large measuring cup, add vegetable oil, vinegar, and sugar. Whisk together

Pour oil mixture over the coleslaw mix and toss everything together until everything is coated well

Cover bowl with plastic wrap and chill in refrigerator for up to 2 hours if desired

Serve cold or room temperature

Parsley Salad with Almonds and Apricots

Cook time: 50 minutes
Servings: 4
Cost per serving: $1.07

1.5 cups cooked and cooled rice
1 bunch flat leaf parsley
1/2 cup sliced almonds
10 dried apricots (about 1/2 cup)
2 tablespoon olive oil
2 tablespoon vegetable or canola oil
2 tablespoon apple cider vinegar
1 clove garlic, minced
1/2 tablespoon dijon mustard
1/2 teaspoon sugar
Salt and pepper to taste

Cook the rice, then spread it out onto a baking sheet or dish and transfer to the refrigerator to cool.

While the rice is cooking, make the dressing so the flavors have time to blend. Mince a clove of garlic and combine it in a bowl with the olive oil, vegetable oil, vinegar, dijon, sugar, salt, and pepper. Whisk the mixture until combined. Set the dressing aside.

Rinse the parsley well with cool water and shake off as much water as possible. Use a salad spinner or pat with a paper towel to remove excess moisture. Roughly chop the leaves, leaving the bottom of the stems behind. Place the chopped parsley in a large bowl. Roughly chop the dried apricots into small pieces. Add the chopped apricots and sliced almonds to the bowl with the parsley. Finally, add the cooked and cooled rice. Pour half of the dressing over top of the salad ingredients and toss until everything is well mixed and coated with dressing. Add more dressing if desired.

Roasted Vegetable Couscous

Cook time: 55 minutes
Servings: 8
Cost per serving: $0.98

4 Roma tomatoes
2 zucchini
1 bell pepper
1 red onion
4 cloves garlic
2 tablespoon olive oil
Salt and pepper to taste
2 cups couscous
3 cups vegetable broth
1/4 bunch parsley

Preheat the oven to 400°F. Wash and chop the tomatoes, zucchini, bell pepper, and red onion into 1 to 1.5-inch pieces. Peel four cloves of garlic but leave them whole.

Toss the chopped vegetables and garlic with olive oil. Spread them out on a baking sheet so they are in a single layer. Sprinkle salt and pepper over the vegetables.

Place the vegetables in the oven and roast at 400°F for about 45 minutes, stirring twice throughout, until the vegetables are wilted and browned on the edges.

While the vegetables are roasting, cook the couscous. Add the vegetable broth to a sauce pot, place a lid on top, and bring to a boil over high heat. Once boiling, add the couscous, turn off the heat, and cover the pot with the lid once again. Let the couscous sit, undisturbed, for ten minutes. Then, fluff with a fork.

After the vegetables are finished roasting, collect the four garlic cloves, and chop them well, then roughly chop the fresh parsley. Combine the couscous, roasted vegetables (including garlic), and parsley in a bowl, and stir to combine. Season with more salt and pepper if desired. Serve warm or cold.

Kale Salad with Toasted Pita and Parmesan

Cook time: 30 minutes
Servings: 4
Cost per serving: $1.28

8 cups shredded kale, loosely packed (about one bunch)

1 whole wheat pita
1/2 tablespoon olive oil
1/4 cup chopped walnuts
1/3 cup golden raisins
1/3 cup shredded or grated Parmesan
1/3 cup champagne vinaigrette

Pull the kale leaves from the stems. Take a handful at a time in one fist, then carefully pull back your fingers one inch at a time as you slice the bunched kale into fine shreds. Place the shredded kale in a colander and rinse well. Allow the kale to dry as you prepare the remaining ingredients.

Cut the pita into 1-inch triangles. Place the pita triangles in a small bowl and drizzle with olive oil. Toss the pita until it is well coated in oil. Heat a small skillet over medium, then once the skillet is hot, add the pita. Cook and stir the pita until they are toasted and crunchy. Remove the pita from the skillet, then add the chopped walnuts. Stir and cook the walnuts in the dry skillet for 1-2 minutes, or just until they begin to smell toasty. Remove them from the skillet immediately to prevent burning.

To assemble the salad, place the washed and dried kale in a large bowl. Add the toasted pita, walnuts, Parmesan, and golden raisins. Pour the champagne vinaigrette over top, then toss until everything is coated in dressing and Parmesan.

Serve the salad immediately, or let it rest for 10-15 minutes to allow the dressing to slightly soften the kale.

Torn Cabbage Salad with Apples and Parmesan

Cook time: 15 minutes
Servings: 8
Cost per serving: $0.81

1 small head of green cabbage
1 crisp apple
2 oz. Parmesan cheese
1/4 cup grainy mustard
2 tablespoons apple cider vinegar
1 tablespoon honey
1/4 cup extra-virgin olive oil
Salt and pepper to taste
1/4 cup or so chopped fresh parsley

> Peel off the first one or two layers of the cabbage until it looks unblemished. Carefully cut out the core from the bottom of the head of cabbage. Cut off the really thick ribs on the outside, towards the bottom of the head. Now rip apart the head, and tear through the leaves, ripping and separating, until all the pieces are

no bigger than 3" long and none should require a knife to eat. Set aside.

Mix the mustard, honey and vinegar in a small bowl and add a pinch of salt and pepper. Whisk in the olive oil while slowly drizzling it in. Taste, and add a bit more of any ingredient if you like to your own taste.

Cut the apple flesh away from the cores. Finely slice the apple into slivers. Finely cut the pecorino, and then cut into matchsticks (or keep as bigger slices if you like).

Combine the apples, pecorino, cabbage and parsley in a large bowl and toss together with the dressing just before serving. Serve immediately.

Bacon and Spinach Salad with Dijon

Cook time: 20 minutes

Servings: 4

Cost per serving: $1.25

1 pound baby spinach leaves
8 slices cooked bacon, crumbled with 3 tablespoon drippings reserved
1 small red onion, thinly sliced
4 eggs, hard boiled and sliced
3 ounces crumbled blue cheese
2 teaspoon sugar
1 teaspoon spicy brown or Dijon mustard

3 tablespoon red wine vinegar
1/2 teaspoon dried thyme
Salt and pepper to taste

In a large mixing bowl, toss the baby spinach, crumbled bacon, thinly sliced red onion, hard boiled egg slices and crumbled blue cheese. In a resealable glass container, add warm bacon drippings with the sugar, spicy or Dijon mustard, red wine vinegar, dried thyme and a pinch of salt and pepper. Shake vigorously. Pour the warm Bacon Vinaigrette over the salad, serve chilled

Zucchini and Orzo Salad

Cook time: 30 minutes
Servings: 4
Cost per serving: $1.25

1 cup orzo pasta
2 tablespoon olive oil
1 teaspoon red wine vinegar
1 medium zucchini, diced
1 medium yellow squash, diced
1 pint grape tomatoes, halved
Salt and pepper, to taste
Fresh basil (optional)

Cook the orzo according to package directions. Drain.

In a medium skillet, add olive oil and red wine vinegar and sauté diced zucchini, diced yellow squash and halved tomatoes for 4 to 5 minutes, stirring occasionally.

Toss the cooked vegetables with the orzo.

Chill up to two hours in the refrigerator before serving.

Apple and Pear Salad

Cook time: 20 minutes

Servings: 8

Cost per serving: $1.04

4 medium apples, thinly sliced

2 medium pears, thinly sliced

1 medium cucumber, seeded and chopped

1 medium red onion, halved and thinly sliced

1/4 cup apple cider or juice

1 tablespoon fresh dill

1 tablespoon olive oil

1 tablespoon spicy brown mustard

2 teaspoons brown sugar

1/2 teaspoon salt

1/4 teaspoon pepper

In a large bowl, combine apples, pears, cucumber and onion. In a small bowl, whisk remaining ingredients until blended. Pour over apple mixture and toss to coat. Refrigerate until serving.

California Pasta Salad

Cook time: 15 minutes

Servings: 15

Cost per serving: $0.94

1 pound thin spaghetti, broken into 1-inch pieces
3 large tomatoes, diced
2 medium zucchini, diced
1 large cucumber, diced
1 medium green pepper, diced
1 sweet red pepper, diced
1 large red onion, diced
2 cans (2-1/4 ounces each) sliced ripe olives, drained
1 bottle (16 ounces) Italian salad dressing
1/4 cup grated Parmesan cheese
1 tablespoon sesame seeds
2 teaspoons poppy seeds
1 teaspoon paprika
1/2 teaspoon celery seed
1/4 teaspoon garlic powder

Cook pasta according to package directions; Drain and rinse in cold water. Transfer to a large bowl. Add the vegetables and olives.
In a large bowl, whisk the dressing ingredients. Drizzle over spaghetti mixture; toss to coat.

Cover and refrigerate up to 12 hours. Serve with a slotted spoon.

Barbeque Chicken

Cook time: 40 minutes
Servings: 4
Cost per serving: $1.04

4 bone-in Chicken Breast Halves
3 tablespoons olive oil
1 1/2 teaspoons smoked paprika
2 tablespoons fresh lemon juice
3 cloves garlic minced
Salt pepper to taste
1 cup prepared BBQ sauce

    Remove skin from chicken breast halves and place in a large ziplock bag.

    Combine olive oil, smoked paprika, lemon juice, and garlic in a small bowl and pour over chicken.

    Let chicken marinade for at least an hour, up to 24 in the fridge.

    Preheat oven to 350 degrees

    Remove chicken from bag and place on a baking sheet. Season with salt and pepper.

    Bake for 20 minutes and brush a layer of BBQ sauce on the chicken. Return to oven and repeat brushing with BBQ sauce every 5 minutes until the chicken is cooked through, about 15 to 20 minutes longer. Chicken is done when it reaches an internal temperature of 165°F when read with a thermometer inserted into thickest part of the breast.

Cheesy Steak Tacos

Cook time: 20 minutes
Servings: 4
Cost per serving: $1.24

3/4 cup shredded cheddar cheese, divided
1 packet taco seasoning
1 New York strip steak
1/4 stick butter
Diced tomato, for topping
Sour cream, for topping
Lime zest to taste (optional)

Preheat oven to 375°F. Line a sheet pan with parchment paper or a Silpat. Set out four glasses that are similar in height and rest a wooden cooking spoon over each pair of glasses. These suspended spoons will be used to shape the tortillas.

Divide cheese into three mounds on top of lined sheet pan. Use hand to flatten and spread cheese into circles spaced 1-2 inches apart.

Bake for 10-15 minutes, or cheese appears lacy and is golden-brown on the edges.

Use a spatula to carefully drape tortillas over suspended spoons to create tortilla shape. Allow to dry and harden.

Meanwhile, sprinkle taco seasoning over both sides of the steak. You may not use the whole packet.

Preheat a grill or grill pan to medium-high. If using a grill pan, melt butter over the top and allow to brown slightly. For medium rare or medium steak, cook for 2-3 minutes. Rotate steak 90 degrees using a fork, and cook for an additional 2-3 minutes. Flip steak with a fork, and repeat process. Remove steak onto a plate and allow to rest for 10-15 minutes, before slicing into thin strips against the grain.

To assemble, fill taco shells with pinch of lettuce, a few strips of steak, a dollop of sour cream, a smattering of diced tomato and avocado, a few thin slices of jalapeño, and a dash of lime zest.

Creamy Chicken Pasta

Cook time: 30 minutes
Servings: 5
Cost per serving: $1.52

- 2 cups uncooked penne pasta
- 1 cup sliced green onions
- 2 tablespoons butter
- 1/2 cup chicken broth
- 1 teaspoon minced garlic
- 1 tablespoon all-purpose flour
- 1/3 cup water
- 1 cup milk
- 2 cups cubed cooked chicken
- 2 tablespoons capers, drained
- 1/4 teaspoon salt
- 1/8 teaspoon pepper
- Parmesan cheese to taste

Cook pasta according to package directions. Meanwhile, in a large skillet, saute and onions in butter for 4-5 minutes or until tender. Add broth and garlic. Bring to a boil; cook until liquid is reduced by half, about 5 minutes. Combine flour and water until smooth; gradually add to mushroom mixture. Bring to a boil. Reduce heat; cook and stir for 2 minutes or until thickened. Stir in cream. Bring to a boil. Reduce heat; simmer, uncovered, for 4-5 minutes or until heated through.

Drain pasta. Add the pasta, chicken, capers, salt and pepper to cream sauce. Cook for 3-4 minutes or until heated through. Sprinkle with Parmesan cheese.

Chicken Pot Pie

Cook time: 20 minutes

Servings: 4

Cost per serving: $1.02

4 frozen buttermilk biscuits

1 1/2 cup chicken stock

1 cup whole milk

3 tablespoon all-purpose flour

1 1/2 teaspoon poultry seasoning

1 chopped small onion

1 cup chopped carrots

3 tablespoon butter

2 cups shredded rotisserie chicken

1 cup frozen cut green beans

2 tablespoon chopped fresh flat-leaf parsley

Biscuits, for serving

Prepare 4 frozen buttermilk biscuits according to package directions.

Meanwhile, in a large mason jar, shake together chicken stock, whole milk, flour, and poultry seasoning. Cook onion and carrots in butter in a large saucepan over medium-high heat until softened, 2 to 3 minutes. Slowly whisk in milk mixture. Bring to a boil, reduce heat, and simmer, stirring often, until thickened, 6 to 8 minutes.

Stir in shredded rotisserie chicken, green beans, and flat-leaf parsley and cook until warm, 4 to 5 minutes. Season with kosher salt and black pepper. Serve topped with biscuits

Taco Sloppy Joes

Cook time: 25 minutes
Servings: 6
Cost per serving: $0.97

1 pound lean ground beef
1 medium onion, chopped
2 cloves garlic, minced
1 packet taco seasoning
1 cup chunky salsa
1/4-1/2 cup water
6 buns, for serving

> Brown ground, chopped onion, and garlic in a large skillet over medium high heat. Drain grease and add the taco seasoning and salsa. Reduce heat to medium low and cook for about 5 more minutes until mixture has thickened and is heated through.
>
> Add up to 1/2 cup of water to achieve desired consistency.
>
> Serve over hamburgers buns and add desired toppings.

Roasted Parmesan Chicken and Tomatoes

Cook time: 25 minutes

Servings: 4

Cost per serving: $1.20

4 boneless, skinless chicken breast fillets

Salt and black pepper to taste

1/4 cup panko breadcrumbs

1/4 cup grated Parmesan

1 tablespoon olive oil

1 tablespoon chopped fresh flat-leaf parsley

1 chopped garlic clove

1 teaspoon Dijon mustard

1 lb. Campari Tomatoes

> Preheat oven to 450°F. Arrange chicken breast fillets on an aluminum foil-lined baking sheet. Season with kosher salt and black pepper. Stir together panko breadcrumbs, grated Parmesan, olive oil, chopped parsley, and chopped garlic clove. Spread Dijon mustard on each chicken breast. Sprinkle with breadcrumb mixture.
>
> Arrange Campari tomatoes around chicken. Bake until chicken is just cooked through, 14 to 16 minutes. Serve with a side salad and garlic bread.

French Onion Chicken Casserole

Cook time: 45 minutes

Servings: 12

Cost per serving: $0.78

3 cups cooked chicken chopped

1 cup celery chopped (or french style green beans)

1 cup cheddar cheese shredded

1 cup sour cream

1 cup mayo

1 can cream of chicken

1/2 cup slivered almonds

6 oz french fried onions

> Preheat oven to 350 and coat a 9x13 baking dish with cooking spray.
>
> In a large bowl, stir celery, cheese, sour cream, mayo and cream of chicken. Add chicken and almonds. Spoon into dish.
>
> Bake uncovered for 30 minutes. Sprinkle fried onion and cook another 5 minutes. Let stand 5-10 minutes, serve warm.

Cheesy Taco Pasta

Cook time: 35 minutes

Servings: 4

Cost per serving: $0.78

1 pound ground beef
Salt and pepper to taste
1 ounce packet taco seasoning
2 cups water
1 cup jarred mild salsa
8 ounces uncooked rotini pasta
1 1/2 cups shredded Mexican-style cheese

> Preheat a large deep skillet over medium heat.
> Add ground beef and season with salt and pepper.
> Cook, stirring occasionally until cooked thoroughly.
> Drain grease.
> Stir taco seasoning into ground beef then stir in water, salsa and pasta noodles.
> Bring mixture to a boil.
> Stir, cover and reduce heat to a simmer.
> Cook for about 15 minutes until pasta is tender.
> Turn off heat and stir in cheese.
> Season with additional salt and pepper if needed.

Skillet Chicken with Brussels Sprouts and Apples

Cook time: 30 minutes
Servings: 4
Cost per serving: $1.22

1 1/2 lb. boneless, skinless chicken thighs

- 2 teaspoon chopped fresh thyme
- Salt and pepper to taste
- 1 tablespoon canola oil
- 1 (12 ounce) package shredded Brussels sprouts
- 1 sliced apple
- 1/2 sliced red onion
- 1 Chopped Garlic Clove
- 2 tablespoon white balsamic vinegar
- 2 teaspoons brown sugar
- 1/3 cup chopped toasted pecans

Season chicken thighs with fresh thyme, and kosher salt and black pepper. Cook in canola oil in a large skillet over medium-high heat until cooked through, 4 to 5 minutes per side; transfer to a plate.

Add shredded Brussels sprouts, apple, red onion, and garlic clove to skillet. Cook, tossing, until Brussels sprouts are wilted and onion has softened, 5 to 6 minutes. Stir in white balsamic vinegar and brown sugar. Season with kosher salt and black pepper.

Return chicken to pan and top with toasted pecans.

Turkey Enchiladas

Cook time: 40 minutes
Servings: 4

Cost per serving: $1.03

- 8 corn tortillas
- 2 3/4 cup green salsa (salsa verde)
- 1/2 cup lowfat sour cream
- 1/2 cup fresh cilantro
- 8 ounces cooked turkey or chicken breast, diced
- 1 jar roasted red peppers
- 6 oz. low-fat Swiss cheese

Place tortilla stack in the oven and heat oven to 425°F.

In a medium bowl, combine the salsa, sour cream and cilantro. Spread 1/2 cup of mixture on the bottom of 2- to 2 1/2-qt. baking dish.

In second bowl, combine the turkey, peppers and 1 cup of cheese. Remove tortillas from oven. Divide the turkey mixture among the tortillas (a scant 1/2 cup each). Roll up and place seam-side down in the baking dish. Top with the remaining salsa mixture.

Cover with nonstick foil and for 15 minutes. Uncover, sprinkle with the remaining 1/2 cup cheese and bake until the cheese melts, 8 to 10 minutes.